LOOK FOR A BIRD

by Edith Thacher Hurd
Pictures by Clement Hurd

A Science I CAN READ Book

HARPER & ROW, PUBLISHERS
New York, Hagerstown, San Francisco, London

This book is dedicated
to Ernest Brooks,
who first helped me to
look for a bird.

Library of Congress Catalog Card Number: 76–58726
Trade ISBN 0–06–022719-2
Harpercrest ISBN 0–06–022720-6

LOOK FOR A BIRD

Birds are almost everywhere.

And only birds have feathers.

Look in the park.

Look on the pond.

Look in the sky.

Look in the trees.

Listen in the morning.

Listen at night.

Birds are almost everywhere.

THE ROBIN

Robins live in the city.
They live in the country.
They build their nests in trees.
The mother Robin lays one egg
a day for three, four, or five days.
She might not be able to fly
if she carried more than one egg
inside her at one time.
Robins may not hear
or smell a worm.
But they can see worms
when they come out of the ground.

Look for:

Reddish breast, gray-brown
back. Young Robin has
brown spots on chest.

THE BLUE JAY

The Blue Jay, like a squirrel,
hides acorns.
Sometimes it is a noisy bird.
It screams, "Jay, jay, jay,"
from the top of a tree.
Then other birds
look out for a cat down below,
or a hawk in the sky.
Sometimes it is a quiet bird.
When it is close to its nest,
it does not make any noise at all.

Look for:

A big bird. Blue above,
gray below. Blue on wings.
Blue crest.

THE RUBY-THROATED
HUMMINGBIRD

The mother Hummingbird
gathers spiderwebs.
She puts them around her nest
with her long bill.
The spiderwebs
make the nest strong.
They hold the nest in the tree.
A Hummingbird's egg is
as small as a pea.
A Hummingbird baby is
as small as a honeybee.

Look for:

A tiny bird.
Male has red throat.
Wings move so fast they hum.

THE PIGEON

Pigeons are also called Rock Doves.
Long ago Pigeons built
their nests on high cliffs.
Now they often build their nests
on high buildings.
This is a safe place for eggs
in the city.
Both the mother and father Pigeon
sit on the eggs.
Both the mother and father Pigeon
feed their babies.
They feed them with "Pigeon milk."

Look for:

A big bird. Gray-white or brownish, mixed colors. Often people feed them in the park.

THE CARDINAL

The Cardinal is a very red bird.
Even its beak is red.
Its beak is thick and strong.
It is good for cracking seeds.
The mother and father Cardinal
build their nest together.
The mother sits on her eggs
for almost two weeks.
The father helps to feed her.
Nine or ten days after they hatch,
the little birds are big enough
to leave the nest.

Look for:

Male red.
Black patch on face.
Female yellowish-brown.
Both have red crests.

THE CROW

When Crows are nesting
or feeding,
one Crow is always watching.
It calls,
"Caw-caw-caw,"
if it sees a hawk or an owl.
Then all the Crows fly together
to drive the hawk
or the owl away.
Hawks and owls eat Crows' eggs
and baby Crows.

Look for:

A big bird. All black.

THE MOCKINGBIRD

The Mockingbird can
croak like a frog,
chirp like a chicken,
whistle like a policeman,
and sing the songs of many birds.
That is why
it is called a Mockingbird.
Mockingbirds also sing
a beautiful song of their own.
Mockingbirds even sing while
they are flying.
Sometimes they sing
in the moonlight.

Look for:

A gray bird with white
on wings and tail.

THE HERRING GULL

The Herring Gull
has webbed feet.
It is a good swimmer
but not a good diver.
It can drink salt water
or fresh water.
Many, many Herring Gulls
often nest together on one island.
They lay their eggs on rocks,
in seaweed on the shore,
or in little hollows in the sand.

Look for:

White bird with gray wings.
Pink legs. Young gulls
brownish until four years old.

THE DOWNY WOODPECKER

The little Downy Woodpecker is
the smallest woodpecker of all.
But it has a big head
and a strong sharp beak.
Its head and beak are like
a little hammer to make holes
in the bark of a tree.
The Downy Woodpecker
has a long tongue.
The tongue has tiny hooks on it
to catch the insects
that live under the bark
of the tree.

Look for:

White on back.
A little red
on head of male.

THE SCREECH OWL

The Screech Owl builds its nest
in a hole in an old tree.
It sleeps all day.
It hunts at night.
The Screech Owl has big eyes.
It can see in the dark.
The Screech Owl can hear well, too.
It can hear a tiny mouse
running into its tunnel at night.
The Owl is very quiet when it hunts.
Its wings do not make any noise
when it flies.

Look for:

A small brown or gray owl.
Feathers stick up like ears.
Does not hoot. Makes a
little *whe-ee-ee* sound.

THE HOUSE SPARROW

House Sparrows live
all over the world.
They live in the country.
They live in the city.
Often there are more
House Sparrows in a city
than any other bird.
They are noisy birds.
They fight with other birds,
and sometimes steal
parts of their nests
when the other birds are away.

Look for:

A little brown bird in the streets or fields. Male has black bill and black bib.

THE MALLARD DUCK

The mother Duck
sits on her eggs
for almost a month.
When the little Ducks hatch
they stay in the nest
for one day.
Then they follow their mother
to the pond.
They know how to swim right away.
They can swim very fast
when the mother Duck calls
"Quack-quack-quack."

Look for:
Male has shiny green head.
Curly tail feathers.
Female brownish.

THE CHICKADEE

The Chickadee does not
fly away for the winter.
It can almost always find enough
food wherever it is.
It hops and flies
all over the trees.
It sometimes even hangs upside down.
It is looking
for tiny spider eggs, cocoons,
and all kinds of insects.
The Chickadee will sometimes
take nuts and seeds and suet
from your hand.

Look for:

A little round bird.
Black cap. Black bib.
White cheek. Calls,
"Chick-a-dee-dee-dee."

THE BALD EAGLE

The Bald Eagle's head
has only white feathers.
That is why
it is called a Bald Eagle.
Its wings are seven feet wide.
Its nest is called an "aerie."
When the nest is old
it is sometimes so deep
you could stand up in it.
It is so big,
you could lie down in it.
The Bald Eagle goes, "Kar-kar-kar."